Pockets 1

Second Edition

Mario Herrera   Barbara Hojel

PEARSON
Longman

T0383519

Pockets 1, Second Edition

Copyright © 2009 by Pearson Education, Inc.

Pearson Education, 10 Bank Street, White Plains, NY 10606

Staff credits: The people who made up the *Pockets, Second Edition* team, representing editorial, production, design, and manufacturing, are Rhea Banker, Iris Candelaria, Tracey Munz Cataldo, Christine Edmonds, Johnnie Farmer, Nancy Flaggman, Yoko Mia Hirano, Christopher Leonowicz, Judy Li, Linda Moser, Barbara Sabella, Susan Saslow, and Mairead Stack.
Text design: Tracey Munz Cataldo
Text composition: TSI Graphics
Text font: Frutiger Bold
Illustrations: Luis Briseno, Luis Montiel, Mari Rodriguez, and Hugo Miranda Ruiz
Photos: Page 48 (family photos) by Alison Austin; all other photographs by David Mager

---

PEARSON LONGMAN ON THE WEB

Pearsonlongman.com offers online resources for teachers and students. Access our Companion Websites, our online catalog, and our local offices around the world.

Visit us at **pearsonlongman.com**.

ISBN-10: 0-13-603898-0
ISBN-13: 978-0-13-603898-6

Printed in China
26 22

Consultants and Reviewers
Claudia Abraham, Pekitas, Mexico City, Mexico • **Celina Aceves**, Instituto Miguel Ángel, Guadalajara, Mexico • **Laura Acosta**, Colegio Quetzal, Mexico City, Mexico • **Lilia Argumedo,** Colegio Guadalupe, Mexico City, Mexico • **Elvia Badillo Chávez,** Universidad Anáhuac, Facultad de Educación, Centro de Asesoría Pedagógica, Mexico City, Mexico • **Rosa María Buerba Villegas**, ICIF México-Universidad Anáhuac, Mexico City, Mexico • **Consuelo Cadena Soria,** Escuela Mexicana Americana, Mexico City, Mexico • **Olga Calva**, Colegio Británico, Mexico City, Mexico • **Jacqueline Castillo**, CIMAT, Mexico City, Mexico • **Yoon Joung Choi,** Ewha Language School, Seoul, Korea • **Alma Georgina Cruz**, Fernando R. Rodríguez, Mexico City, Mexico • **Ruth Cruz**, Colegio Carmel, Mexico City, Mexico • **María del Consuelo Durán,** Escuela Mexicana Americana, Mexico City, Mexico • **Rosario Escalada**, Universidad Motolinia, Mexico City, Mexico • **Blanca E. García Robledo,** Kinder John F. Kennedy, Guadalajara, Mexico • **Edgar García Ruvalcaba**, Escuela Bertha Von Glummer, Guadalajara, Mexico • **Mónica García,** Instituto Pierre Faure, Guadalajara, Mexico • **Antonieta González**, IFIMAC, Guadalajara, Mexico • **Jennifer Huerta**, Monte Rosa, Mexico City, Mexico • **Irma Isabel Izquierdo**, Colegio Leonardo Da Vinci, Cancun, Mexico • **Ruth Jasso Valtierra**, Colegio Victoria Tepeyac, Mexico City, Mexico • **Helen Jean**, Hansol GEN, EFL R & D Director, Seoul, Korea • **Ana Langarica Rentería,** Centro Escolar del Tepeyac, Mexico City, Mexico • **Eun-Mi Lee**, Mokdong SLP, Seoul, Korea • **Lorena Patricia Lizardo**, Centro Educativo los Pinos, Guadalajara, Mexico • **Laura López de la Vega,** Colegio Miraflores, León, Mexico • **María Inés López**, FORMUS, Monterrey, Mexico • **Juanita Elvira Marroquín,** Instituto Regiomontano, Monterrey, Mexico • **Lucy Miranda**, Liceo Mexicano, Monterrey, Mexico • **Gabriela Muela**, Instituto Olimpia, Monterrey, Mexico • **Aida Nájera**, Bernardo de Balbuena, Mexico City, Mexico • **Margarita Natera**, Colegio Hispano Inglés, Leon, Mexico • **Marcela Reyes**, Colegio Reims, Mexico City, Mexico • **Angélica Ríos**, Nanny, Mexico City, Mexico • **Mariana Serralde**, Centro Educativo Monteverde, Cancun, Mexico • **María Fernanda Torres Romero,** Escuela Mexicana Americana, Mexico City, Mexico • **Bertha Vázquez**, Latin American School, Monterrey, Mexico • **Lucy Vergara**, Colegio Andersen, Mexico City, Mexico

Pearson Longman would like to thank the following schools for piloting *Pockets, Second Edition*:
Colegio Anglo Francés, Monterrey, Mexico • **Colegio Cervantes Colonias**, Guadalajara, Mexico • **Colegio Euterpe**, Monterrey, Mexico • **Colegio Highlands**, Monterrey, Mexico • **Colegio Himalaya**, Monterrey, Mexico • **Colegio Hispanoamericano**, León, Mexico • **Colegio Isabel La Católica**, Monterrey, Mexico • **Colegio Mexicano**, Monterrey, Mexico • **Colegio Mi Pequeño Sol**, León, Mexico • **Colegio Miraflores**, León, Mexico • **Instituto Damicis**, Puebla, Mexico • **Instituto Godwin**, Mexico City, Mexico • **Instituto Kilimanjaro**, Monterrey, Mexico • **Instituto Leonés**, León, Mexico • **Instituto Mexicano Madero, Campus Toledo**, Puebla, Mexico • **Instituto Mexicano Madero, Campus Zavaleta**, Puebla, Mexico • **Instituto Miguel Angel**, Guadalajara, Mexico • **Instituto Olimpia**, Monterrey, Mexico • **Irish Valley Preschool**, Monterrey, Mexico • **Kinder Andes**, Mexico City, Mexico • **Kinder Edelweiss**, Mexico City, Mexico • **Oak Hill CECVAC Preschool**, Monterrey, Mexico • **Oxford Preschool**, Mexico City, Mexico • **Pinecrest Institute**, Mexico City, Mexico

Child Reviewers
Emily Bupp (4 years old) • **Kyle Shigeo Frommer** (4 years old) • **Cole Nam** (3 years old) • **Carlos Portillo Vázquez** (3 years old) • **Karla Portillo Vázquez** (5 years old) • **Marlee Reinmuth** (5 years old) • **Melissa Rodino** (5 years old) • **Veronika J. Volcjak** (3 years old) • **Nina Marie Williams** (4 years old)

Contents

My Classroom

Listen and point. Say.

Warm Up

5 Listen, point, and say. Trace.

glue

red

Presentation: *glue, crayon, paper, door, chair, table*

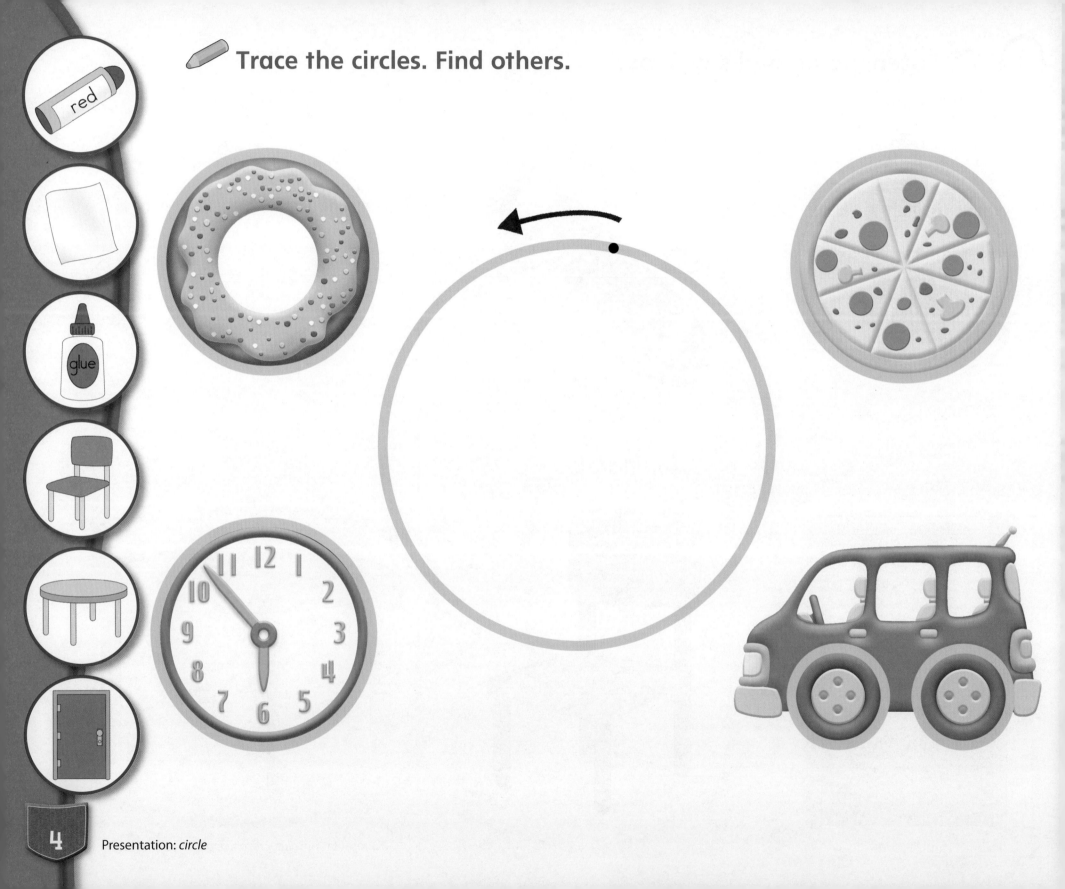

Trace the circles. Find others.

Presentation: *circle*

Draw yourself in the classroom.

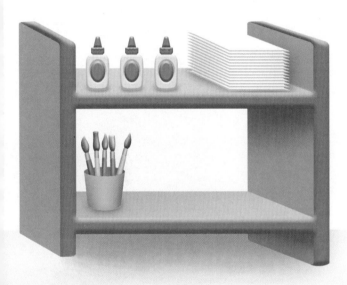

Practice: *classroom people/things*

Stick and color.

Practice: *red*

Trace and say.

Practice: *circle*

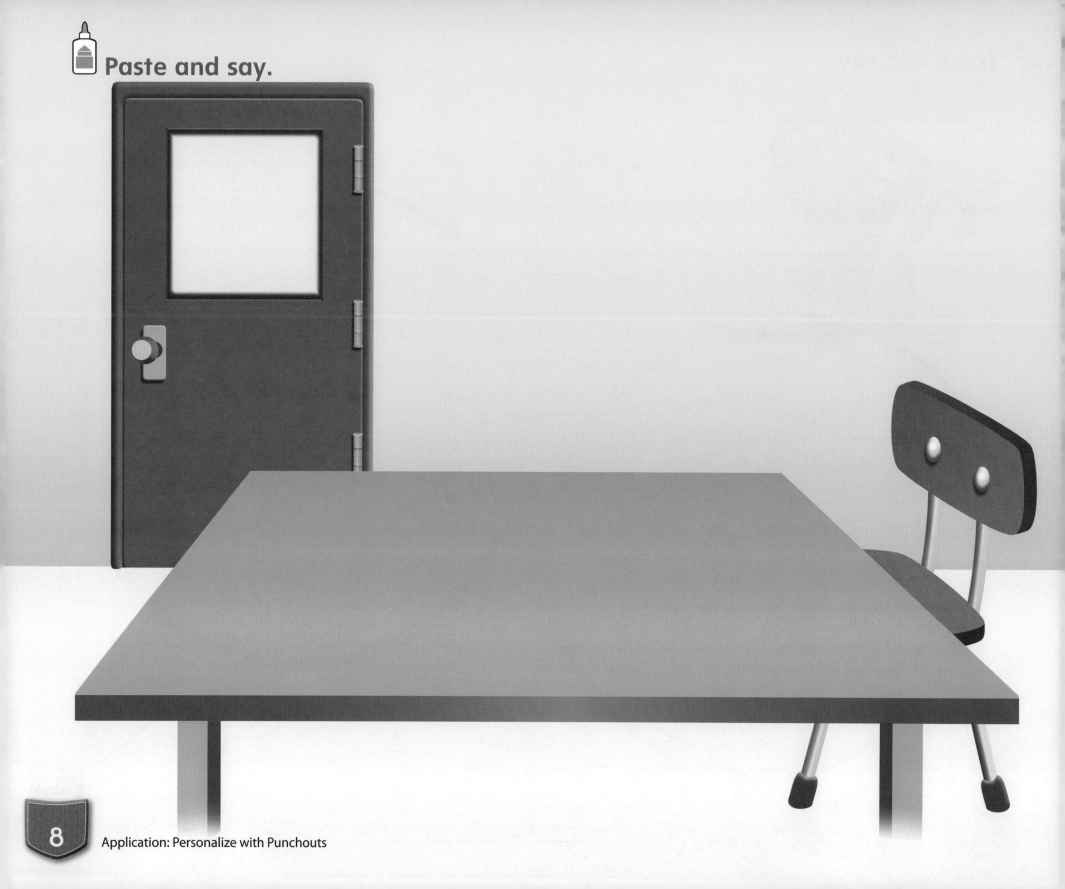

Application: Personalize with Punchouts

At School

Let's read.

Yippee!

Hi! My name is Kim.

Hi! My name is Alex.

Look! It's a crayon.

It's red.

Give me the glue, please.

Yes!

Color the picture frame.

Application: Do What's Right

My Red Door

Draw and paste. Open and close.

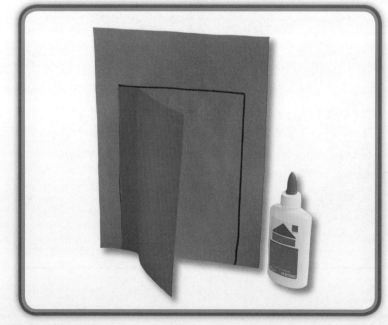

Play and say. Stick.

2 My Body

Listen and point. Say.

16 🎧 ✏️ **Circle the body parts. Say.**

Presentation: *eyes, ears, nose, mouth, arms, legs*

Find and point to the circles.

Practice: *circle*

Trace. Draw your face.

Practice: *body parts/happy, sad*

Stick and color.

18 Practice: *blue*

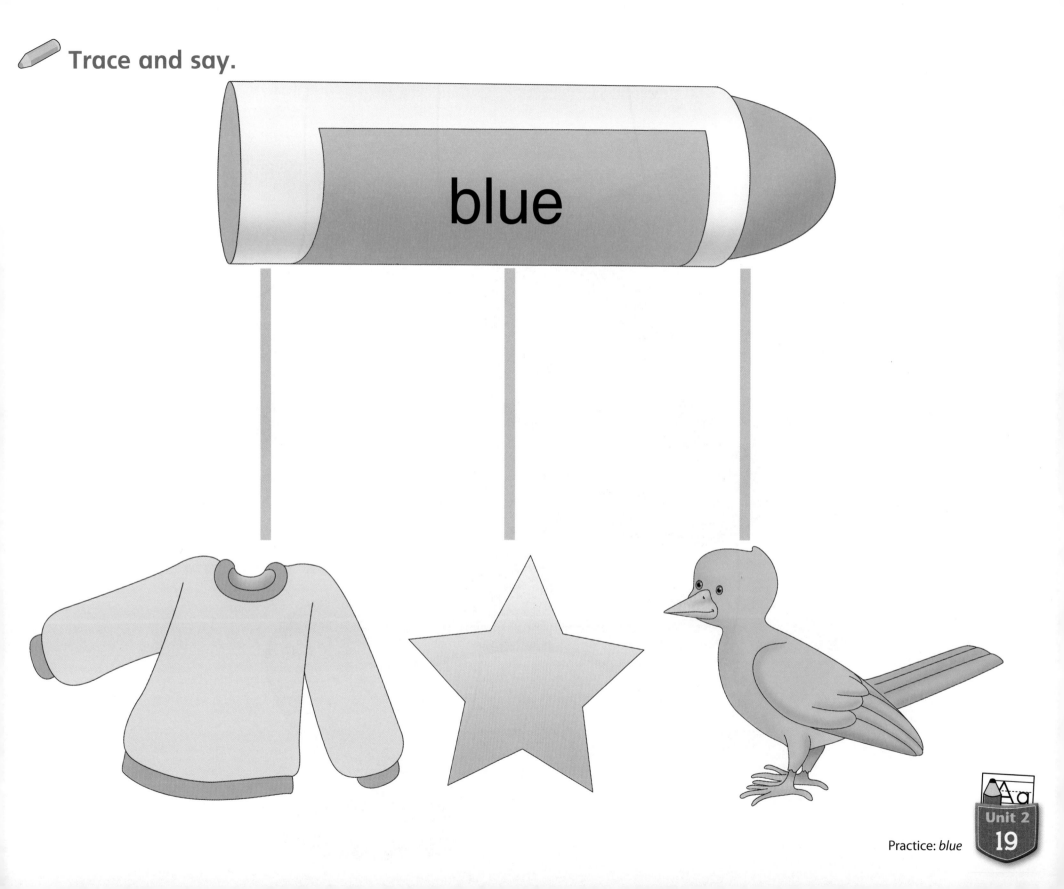

Trace and say.

blue

Practice: *blue*

Paste and say.

Application: Personalize with Punchouts

This is fun!

🎧 22 Look!

Look! This is my nose.

Look! This is my mouth.

2

Look! These are my eyes.

Look! These are my ears.

3

🖊 **Trace and say.**

Wash Your Hands

Values

My Stick Puppet

Draw and paste.

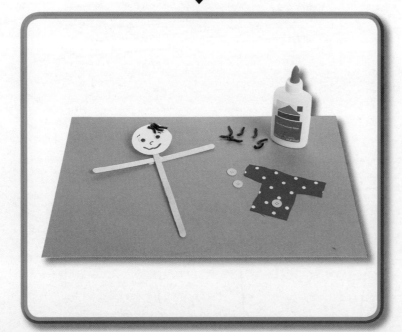

Application: Make a Project

Point to the body parts and say. Stick.

3 My Toys

Listen and point. Say.

Listen, point, and say. Trace.

Presentation: *boat, doll, game, puppet, teddy bear, train*

Trace the squares.

Presentation: *square*

Trace and say.

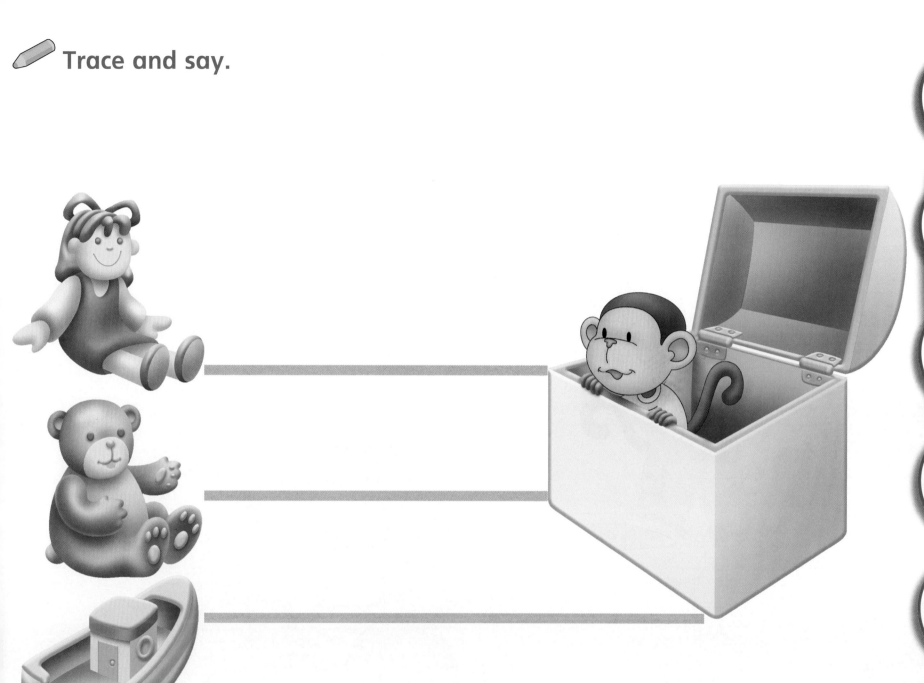

Stick and color.

Practice: *yellow*

Trace the circles.

Practice: *circle*

Paste and say.

Application: Personalize with Punchouts

 **Thank you, Mother!**

 I love my teddy bear!

Oh no! My teddy is broken!

Don't cry. I'll fix it!

OK.

Color the toys and say.

Values

Application: Do What's Right

My Bear

Fold, paste, and draw.

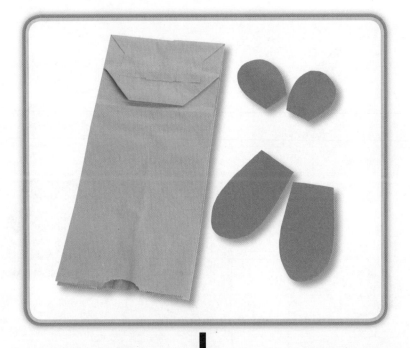

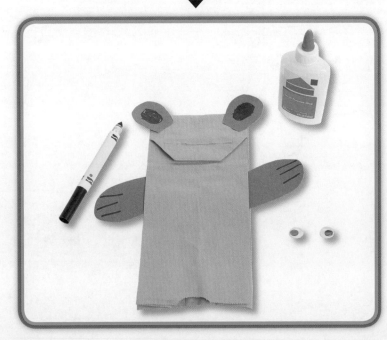

Application: Make a Project

Play and say. Stick.

Unit 3
GOOD JOB!

Unit 3
37

Assessment

Listen and point. Say.

Listen, point, and say. Trace.

Unit 4
39

Presentation: *grandparents, mother, father, sister, brother, baby*

 **Trace the squares.**

Practice: *square*

Trace. Point and say.

Practice: *square/rooms in a house*

Stick and color.

Practice: *green*

Say and color.

red   blue   yellow   red   blue   yellow

Unit 4
43

Practice: *red, blue, yellow*

Paste and say.

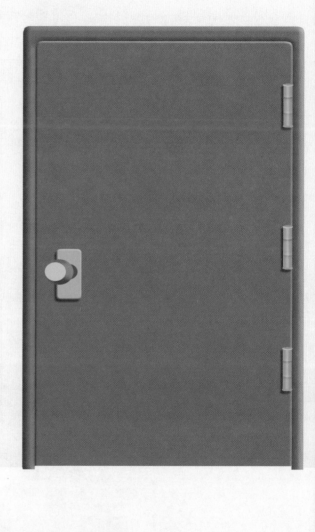

 This is the baby.

 # My Family

 This is my father.

 Hello!

This is my brother.

Hello!

2

This is my sister.

Hello!

3

My Family Album

Fold, paste, and draw.

Application: Make a Project

Unit 4
GOOD JOB!

5 Our Pets

Listen and point. Say.

46 **Listen, point, and say. Trace.**

Presentation: *cat, dog, rabbit, turtle, fish, bird*

Trace the triangles.

Presentation: *triangle*

Draw a line and say.

Practice: *blue, yellow, green/big, little*

Stick and color.

Practice: *orange*

Trace and draw. Say.

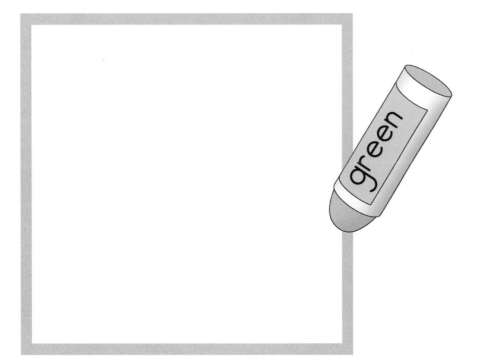

Practice: *colors/square*

Paste and say.

Application: Personalize with Punchouts

Good-bye!

4

54

**Hello, Sam. Look!
I have a dog.**

1

 Hello, Ann. Look! I have a rabbit.

Hello, Ann. Hello, Sam. Look! I have a cat.

Circle the cat. Draw another pet.

Values

Application: Do What's Right

My Rabbit

Use dough and make a pet.

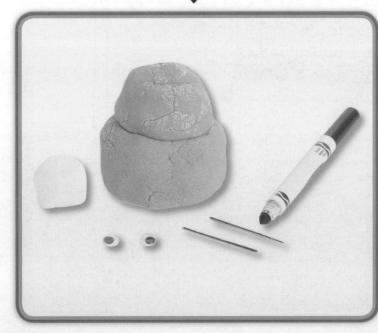

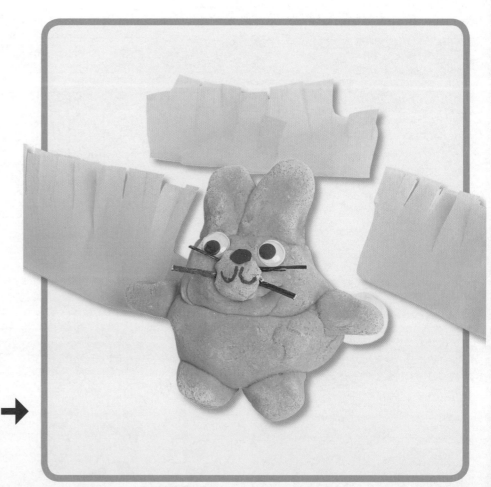

Play and say. Stick.

6 My Clothes

Listen and point. Say.

Listen, point, and say. Trace.

Presentation: *T-shirt, pants, shoes, dress, jacket, pajamas*

✏️ **Trace the triangles. Find others.**

Practice: *triangle*

 **Match the clothes and say.**

Practice: *clothing items*

Stick and color.

Practice: *purple*

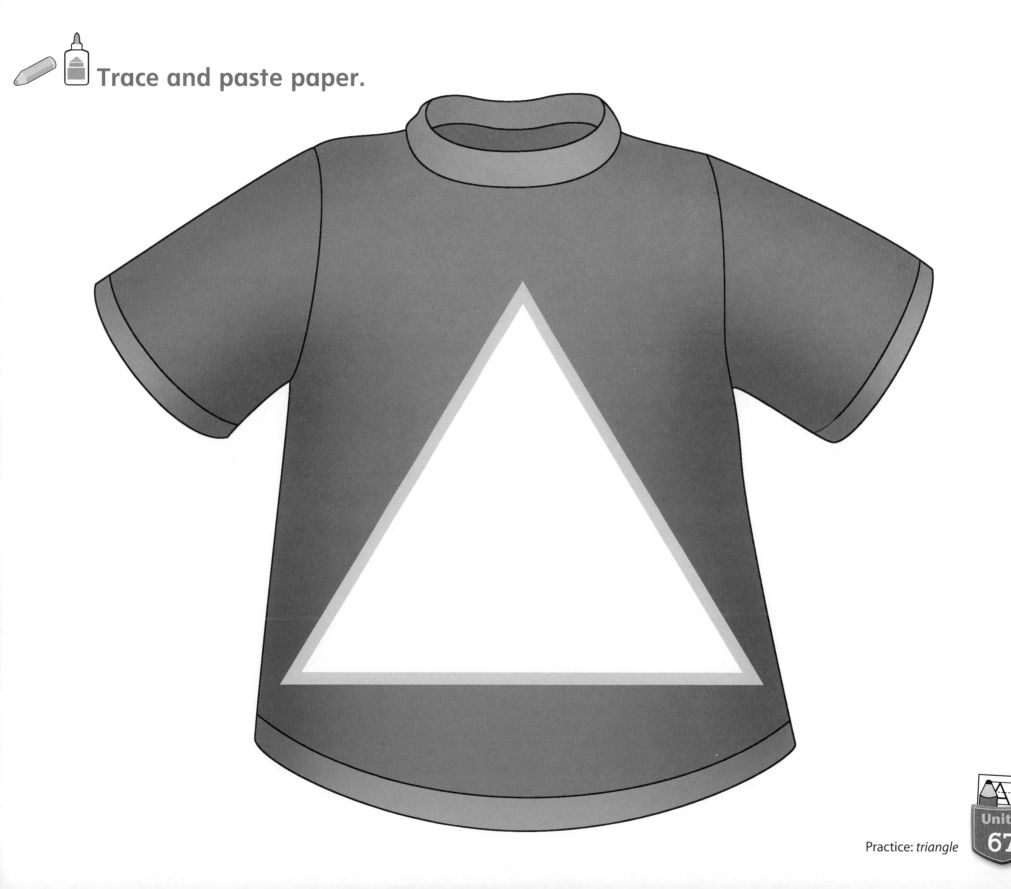

Trace and paste paper.

Practice: *triangle*

Paste and say.

Application: Personalize with Punchouts

Thank you, Mother!

You're welcome.

4

The Red T-Shirt

65

Look, Mother! I want a T-shirt!

1

OK! Let's go in.

Hello! What do you want?

I want a red T-shirt, please

Values

Application: Do What's Right

My T-Shirt

Draw and paste.

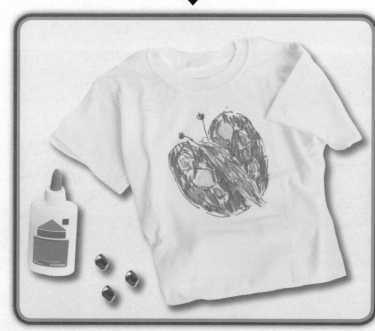

Application: Make a Project

Play and say. Stick.

7 Party Food

Listen and point. Say.

Listen, point, and say. Trace.

Presentation: *cake, ice cream, pizza, sandwich, lemonade, orange juice*

Trace the rectangles. Find others.

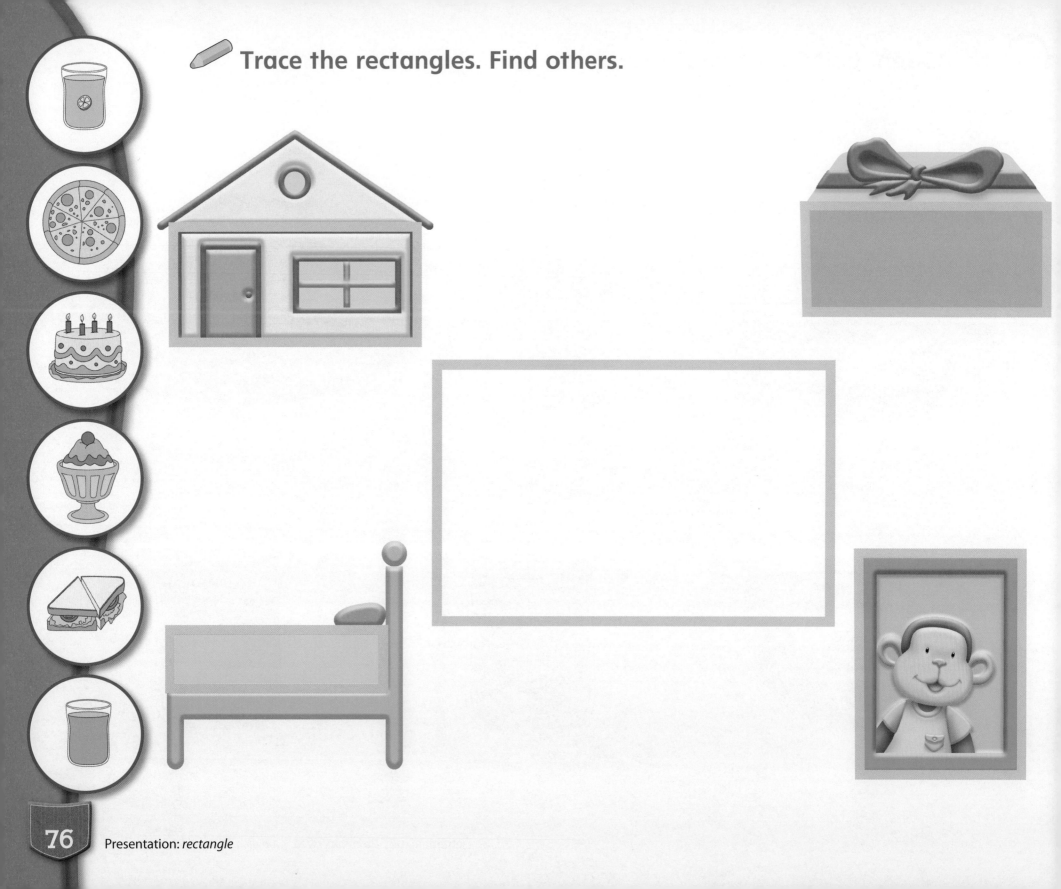

Presentation: *rectangle*

✏️ Draw lines in color and say.

Practice: *blue, yellow, green, orange, purple*

Stick and color.

pink

Practice: *pink*

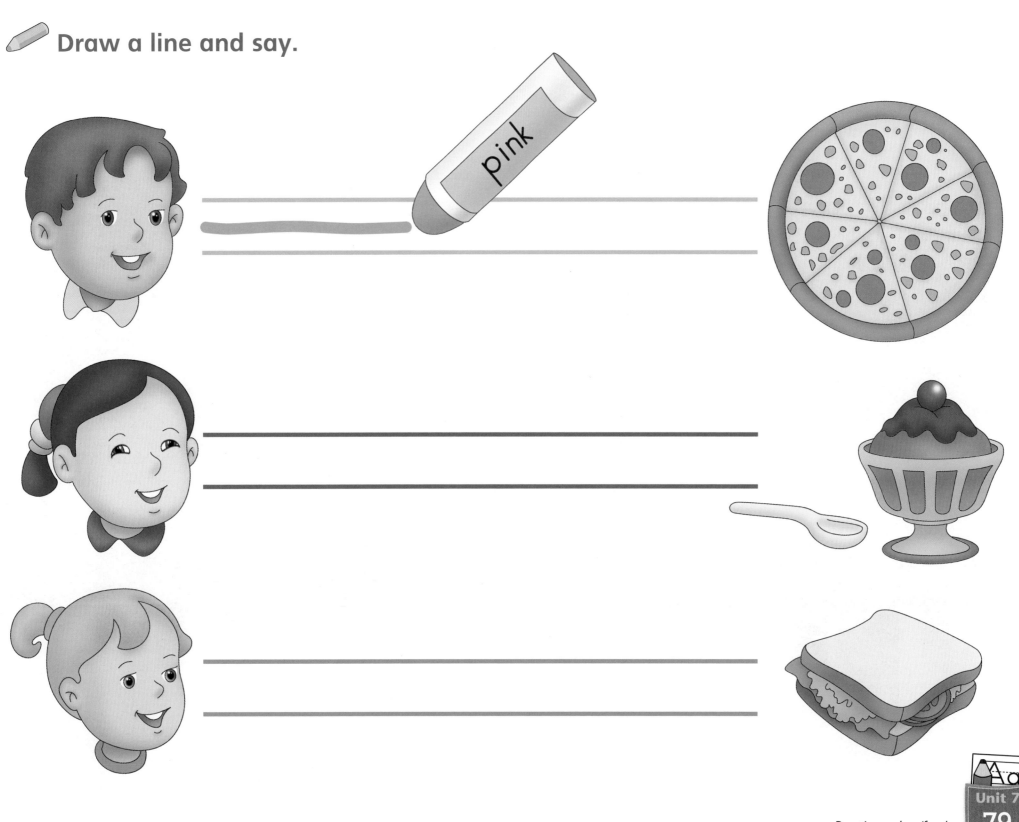

Draw a line and say.

pink

 **Paste and say.**

Application: Personalize with Punchouts

Good-bye, Alex! Thank you!

You're welcome!

Hello! Let's have a party.

4

1

Look, pizza! Lemonade!

2

I like pizza!

I like lemonade!

3

Paste paper on the frame.

Values

My Pizza

Draw and paste.

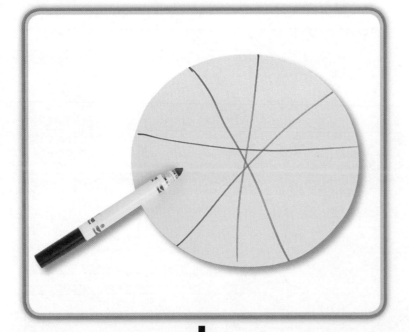

Play and say. Stick.

8 Around My Home

Listen and point. Say.

Presentation: *swings, slide, tricycle, park, apartments, store*

Trace the rectangles. Find others.

Store

Practice: *rectangle*

Match and say.

Practice: *neighborhood things*

Stick and color.

90 Practice: *brown*

Draw a path. Say.

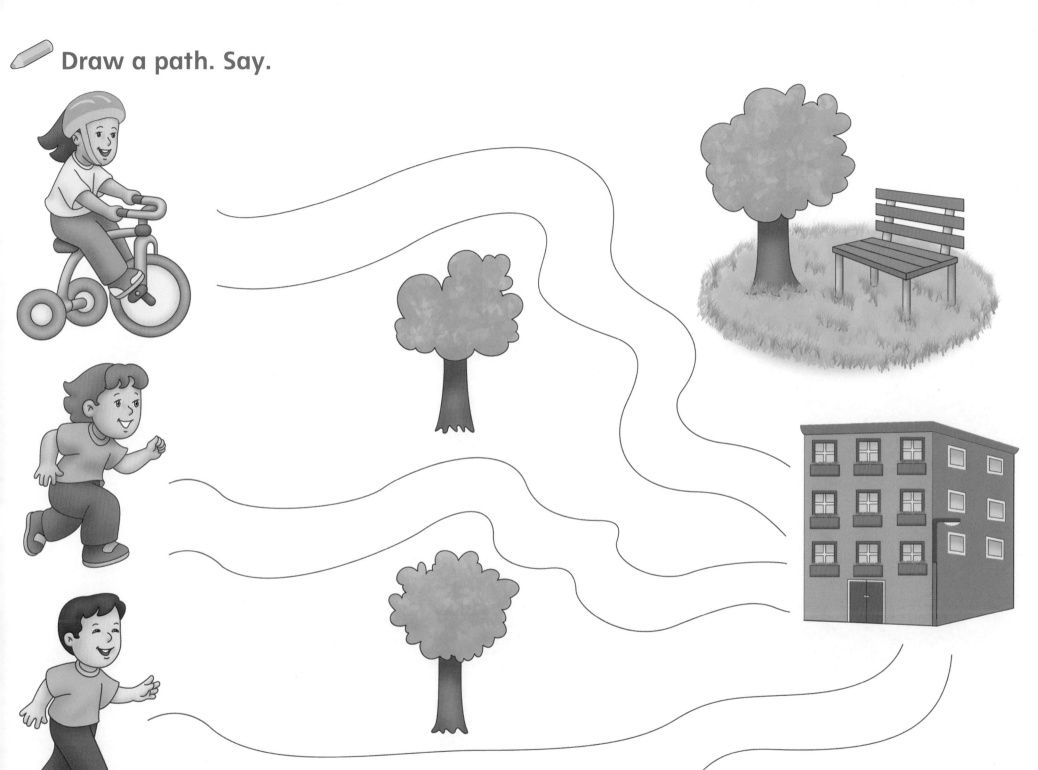

Practice: *actions/neighborhood places*

Paste and say.

Application: Personalize with Punchouts

Thank you, Mother.
We like the park.

Let's go to
the park.

Yes!
Yes!

I like the slide.

Whee!

Let's go to the swings!

Yes! I like swings!

TOYS

FOOD

Trace and say "Hello."

Be Friendly

Our Playground Picture

Draw and paste.

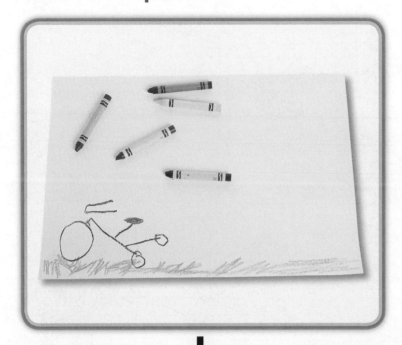

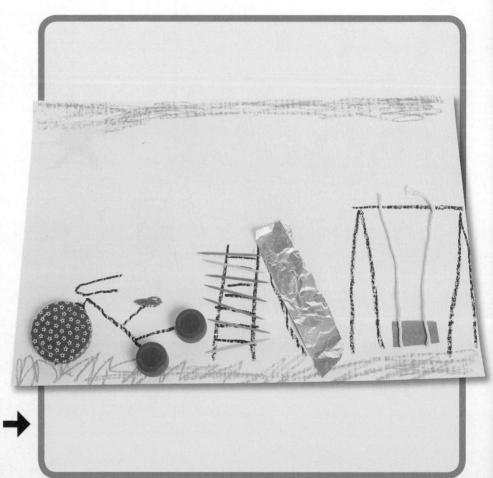

Application: Make a Project

Play and say. Stick.

Store

9 Nature Around Us

Listen and point. Say.

Listen, point, and say. Trace.

Presentation: *tree, grass, sun, flower, bugs, dirt*

Trace and say.

Practice: *circle, square, triangle, rectangle*

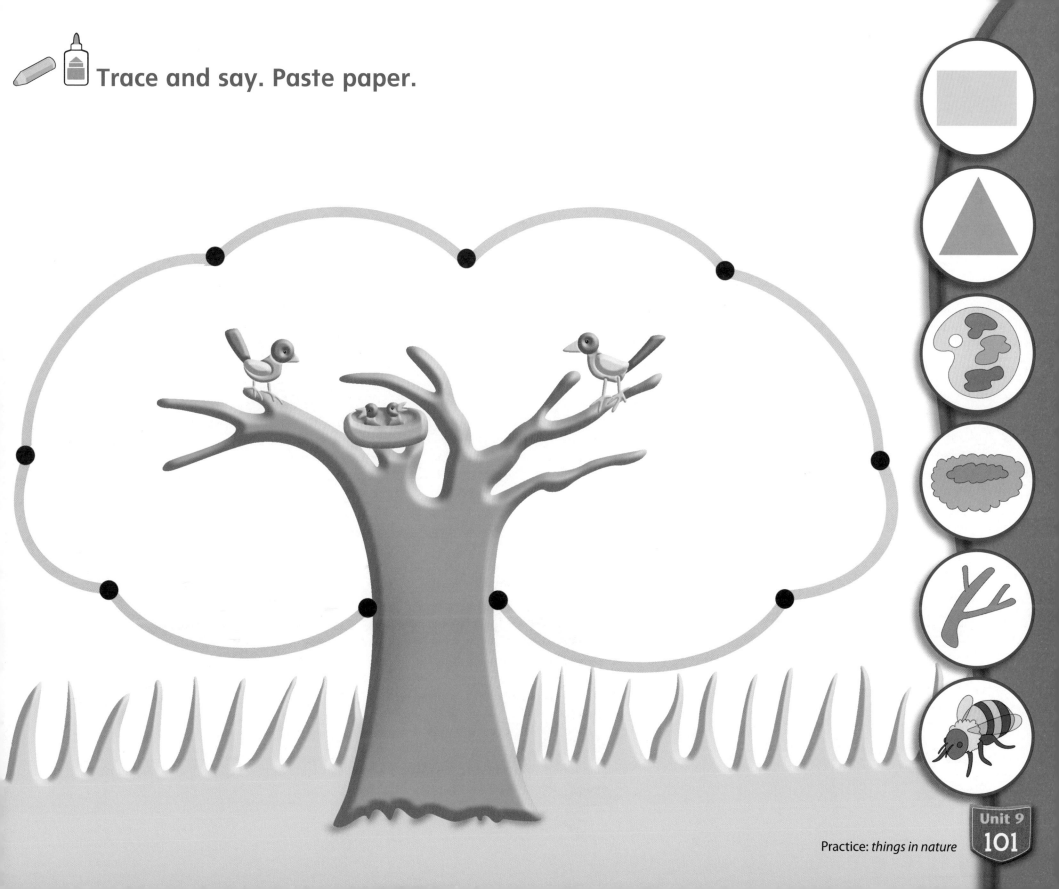

Trace and say. Paste paper.

Practice: *things in nature*

 **Stick and color.**

white

black

Practice: *white, black*

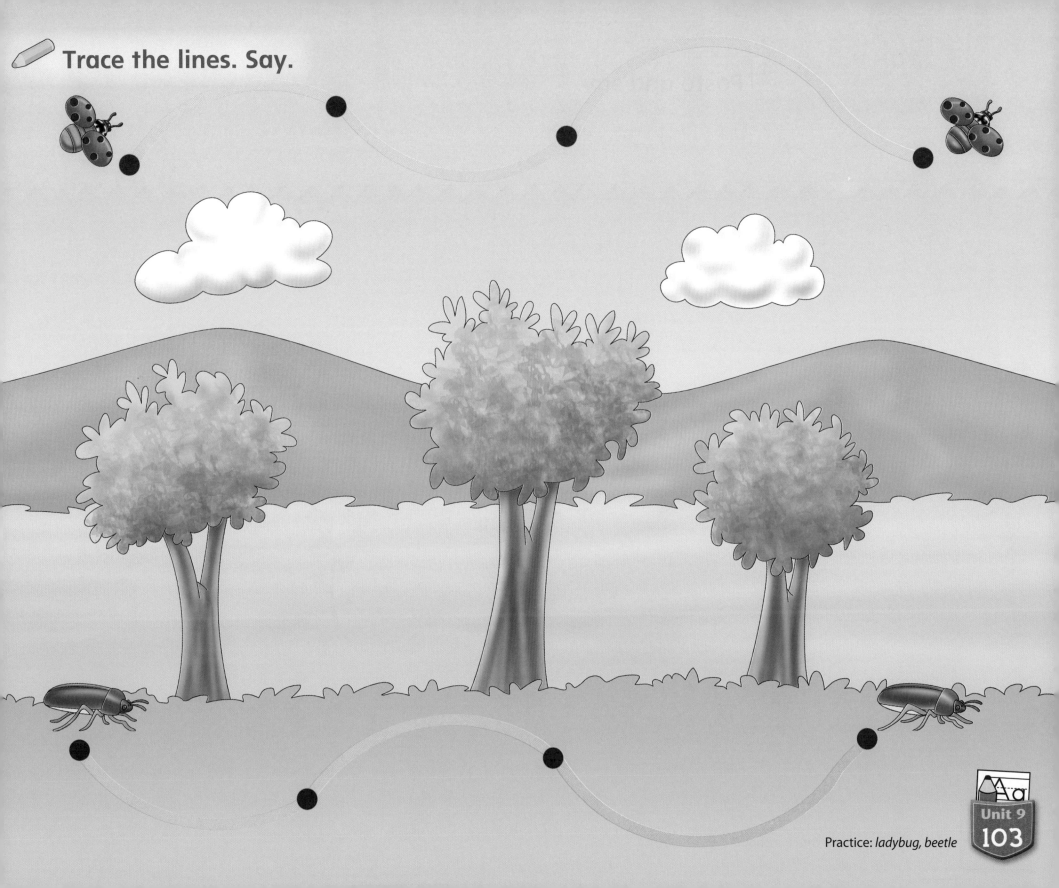

Trace the lines. Say.

Practice: *ladybug, beetle*

 **Paste and say.**

Application: Personalize with Punchouts

Good-bye.

4

Look!

What's that?

1

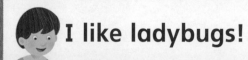 It's a ladybug!

2

 I like ladybugs!

 Wow!

3

Draw more grass and flowers.

Enjoy Nature

Values

Application: Do What's Right

My Ladybug

Color and paste.

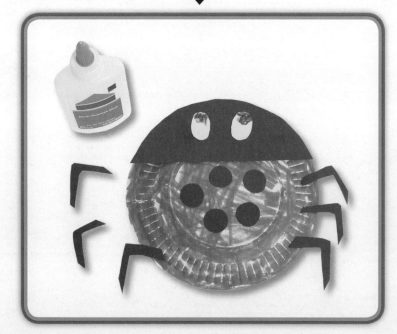

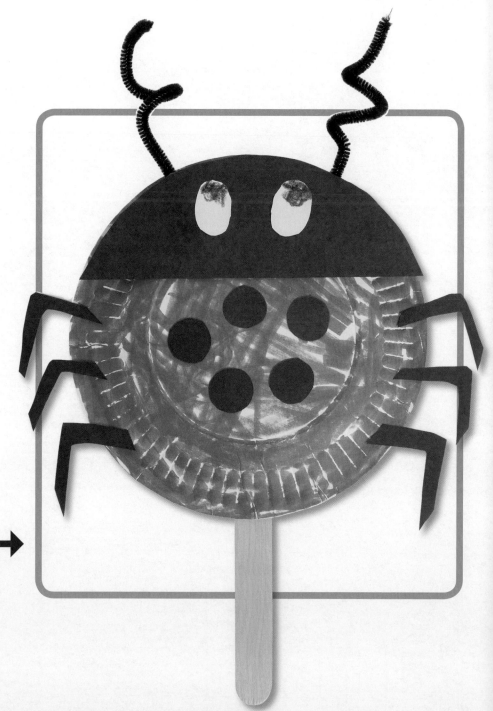

Application: Make a Project

Point and say. Stick.